PIANO

10 jazz standards and original pieces with play-along CD

Alexander L'Estrange and Tom Pilling

© 2005 by Faber Music Ltd
First published in 2005 by Faber Music Ltd
3 Queen Square London WC1N 3AU
Cover by Velladesign
Music processed by MusicSet 2000
Printed in England by Caligraving Ltd

ISBN 0-571-52306-4

CD recorded at Wedgwood Studios, Surrey, January 2005
Engineered by Oliver Wedgwood
Produced by Alexander L'Estrange and Tom Pilling
Guitar: Tom Pilling, Bass: Alexander L'Estrange, Drums: Mike Bradley
℗ 2005 Faber Music Ltd © 2005 Faber Music Ltd

How to use this book

Jazz Sessions is a play-along album with a difference. The CD backings were recorded by real live musicians, so not only do you get to play along with your own band, you can really get an authentic feel for the style. And because improvisation is a key skill for all jazz musicians, each piece in *Jazz Sessions* appears in two versions. Firstly you will find the 'written-out solo' version ready to be played straight through, whilst the second is an extended version for improvisation and experimentation. 'Notebanks' have been included in these versions, to help you get started. Try experimenting with using the pitches in different octaves, and in any order. They are a guide only – of course it is perfectly acceptable to use any of the 12 pitches at any time, as long as they sound right! Experiment with chromatic and whole-tone scales and modes too. Similarly, we have included a suggested left-hand during the solo sections to help you get started. Once you become more advanced, you can work out your own left-hand 'comp'. When you have mastered creating your own melodies from the suggested pitches, you can then begin to follow the chord symbols.

If you want to develop your improvisation skills further, there's no better way than by listening to as much jazz as possible, and copying and experimenting. The essence of jazz is in exploration, and we hope that you enjoy exploring the pieces in this book.

Alexander L'Estrange and Tom Pilling

Wie man dieses Buch benutzt

Jazz Sessions ist ein "Spiel-mit" Album der anderen Art. Die CD-Aufnahmen wurden mit Live-Musikern eingespielt – somit kann man nicht nur mit der eigenen Band spielen, sondern bekommt auch ein echtes Gefühl für den Stil. Und weil Improvisation eine Schlüsselfähigkeit für Jazz Musiker ist, gibt es jedes Stück in *Jazz Sessions* in zwei Versionen. Zuerst findet man die einfache Solo Version, bestens geeignet zum Durchspielen, dann gibt es eine zweite, ausgebaute Version für Improvisation und Experimentieren. 'Notebanks' sind in diesen Versionen enthalten um bei den Anfängen zu helfen. Versuche einfach, mit den Tonhöhen in verschiedenen Oktaven zu experimentieren. Sie sind nur eine Richtlinie – natürlich ist es absolut richtig irgendeine der 12 Tonhöhen zu benutzen, solange sie sich gut anhören! Experimentiere auch mit chromatischen und Ganztonleitern und Tonarten. Ähnlich haben wir hier einen Vorschlag für die linke Hand eingebaut um eine Starthilfe zu geben. Sobald man etwas erfahrener wird, kann man eine individuelle linkshändige Begleitung ausarbeiten. Wenn man die vorgeschlagenen Tonhöhen beherrscht, sollte man anfangen den Akkord Symbolen zu folgen.

Zur Weiterentwicklung der Improvisationsfähigkeiten gibt es keinen besseren Weg als so viel Jazz wie nur möglich zu hören, zu kopieren und zu experimentieren. Das Wesen des Jazz liegt im Erforschen und Entwickeln und wir hoffen, dass man die Stücke in diesem Buch mit Vergnügen spielt.

Alexander L'Estrange und Tom Pilling

CONTENTS

4

C jam blues Duke Ellington arr. Pilling

C jam blues Duke Ellington arr. Pilling

last time to Coda

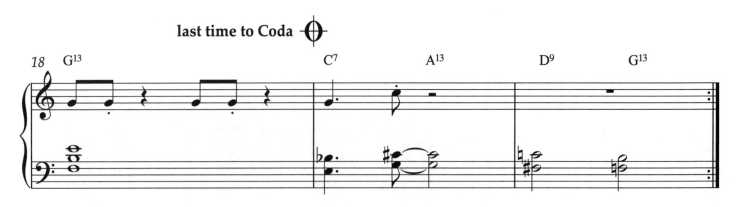

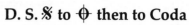

3 **Snowdrop** Tom Pilling

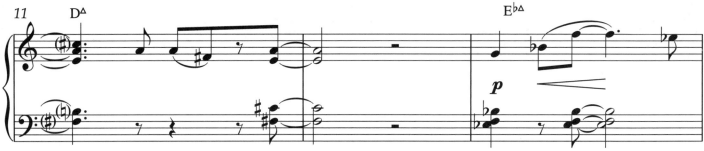

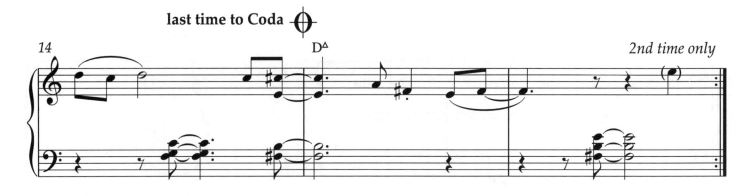

SOLO

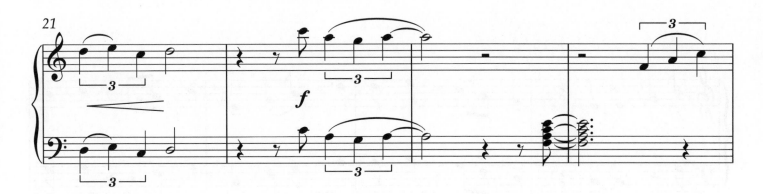

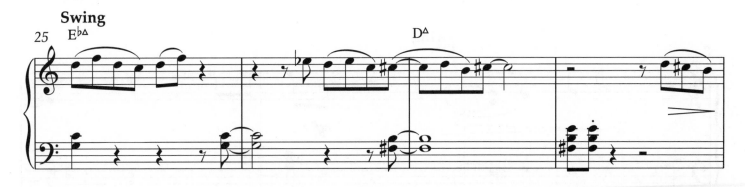

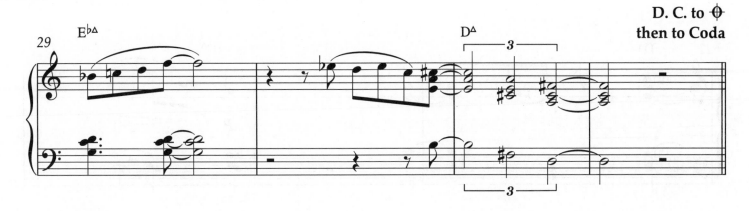

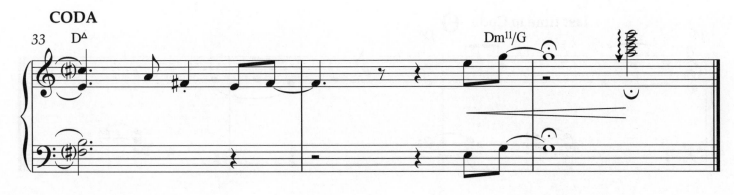

4 Snowdrop Tom Pilling

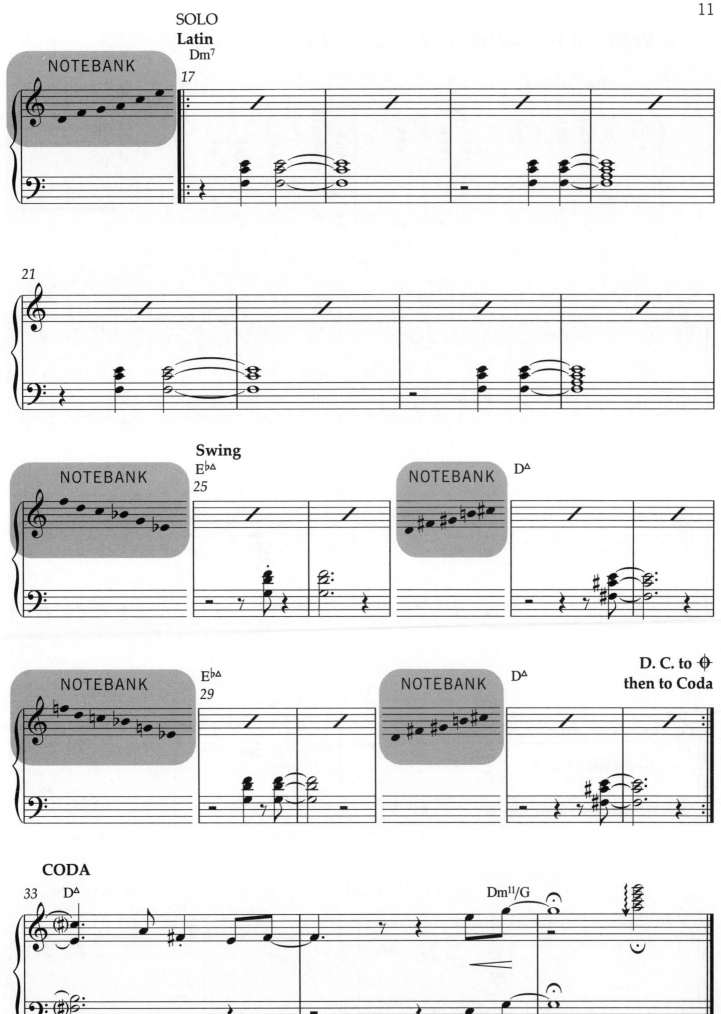

Wade in the water traditional spiritual arr. L'Estrange

Wade in the water traditional spiritual arr. L'Estrange

NOTEBANK

SOLO

D. S. 𝄋 to ⨁ then to Coda

CODA

rall.

Wanna walk with me? Alexander L'Estrange

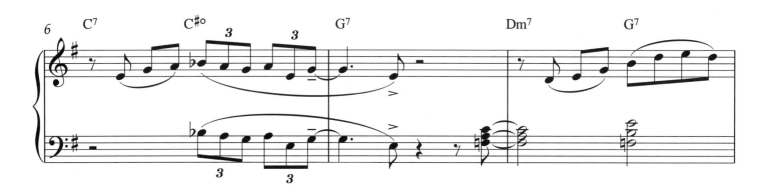

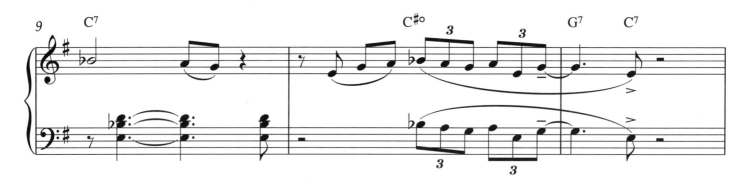

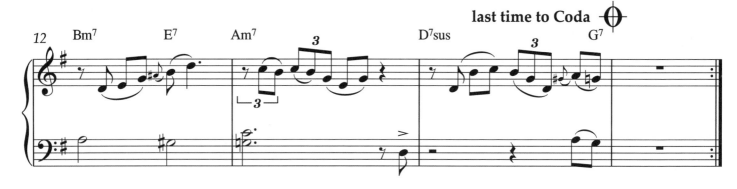

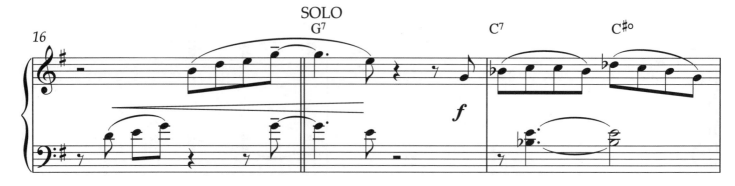

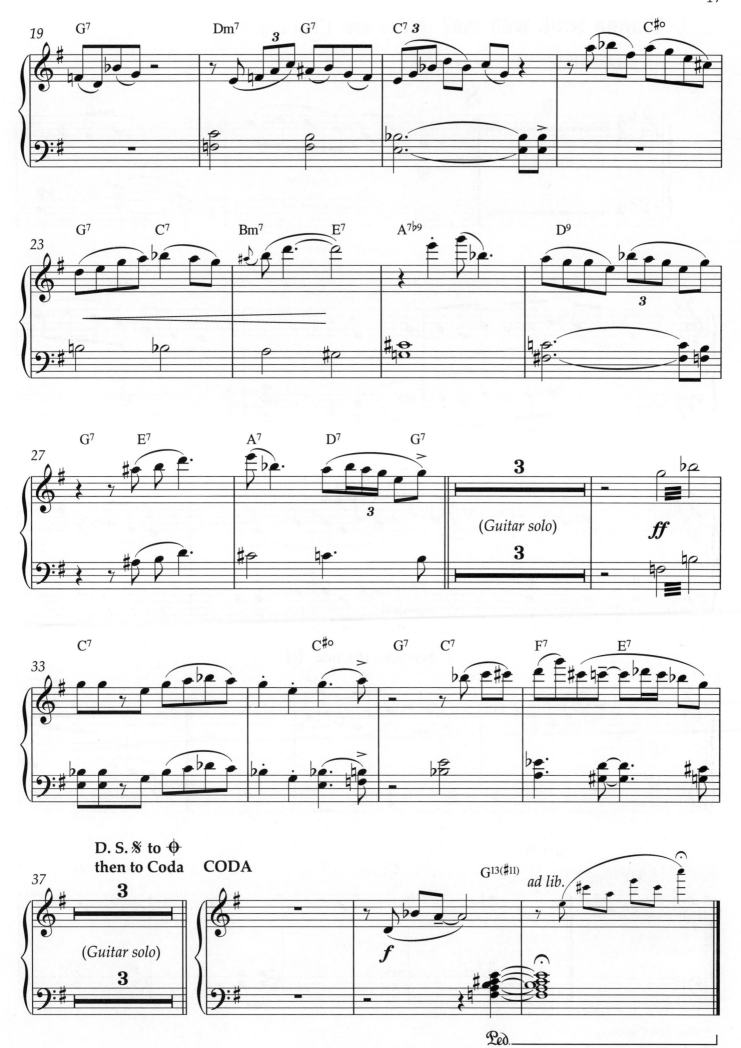

Wanna walk with me? Alexander L'Estrange

Jauntily ♩ = 120

NOTEBANK

SOLO

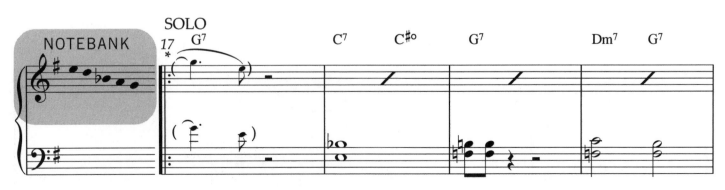

* Play first time only

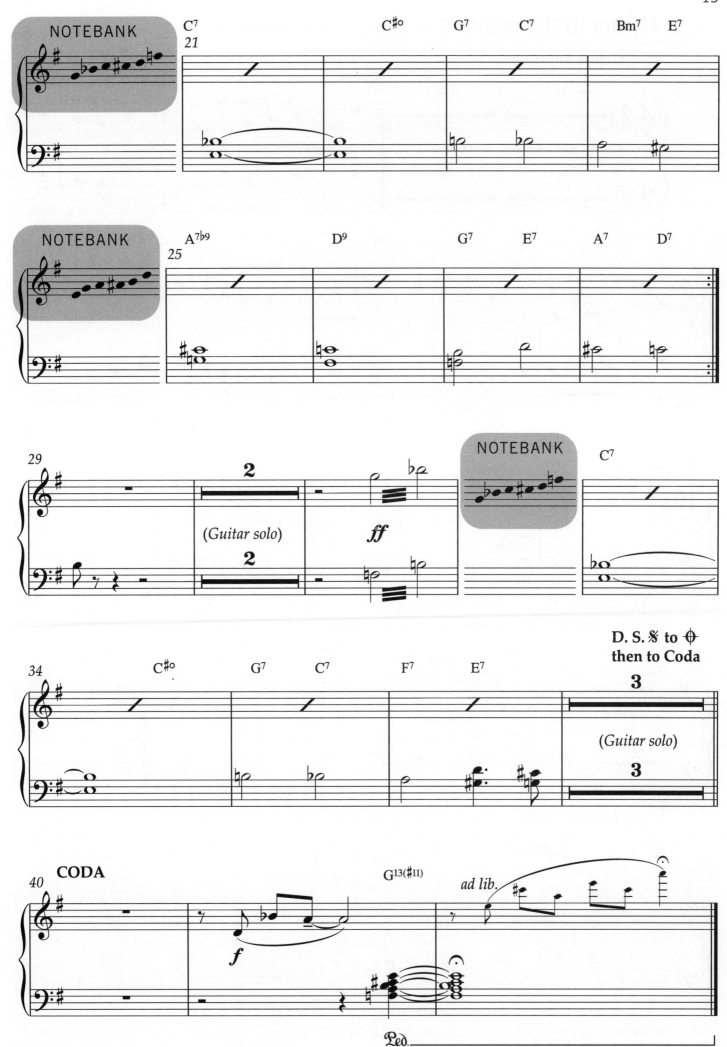

Fly me to the moon   Bart Howard arr. L'Estrange

last time to Coda

SOLO

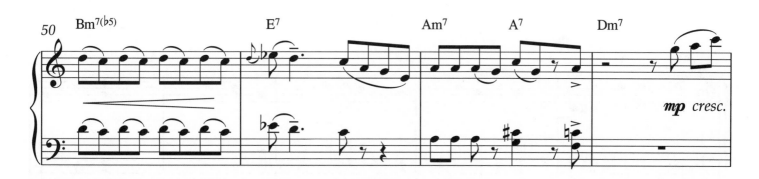

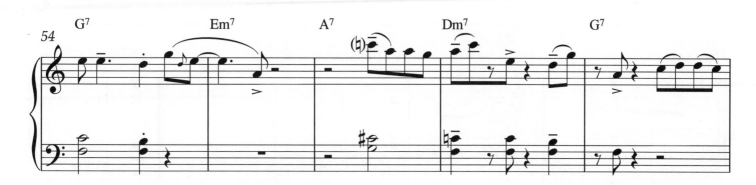

D. S. % to ⊕ (taking 2nd time)
then to Coda   CODA

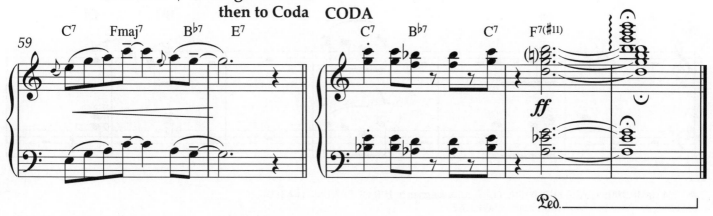

🔟 Fly me to the moon   Bart Howard arr. L'Estrange

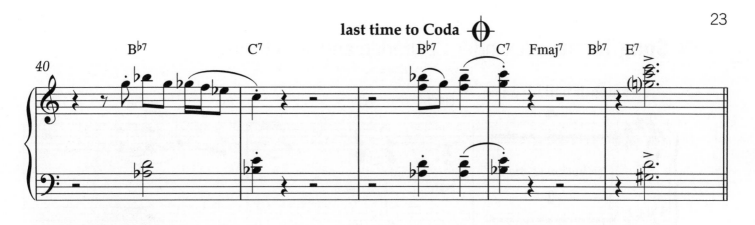

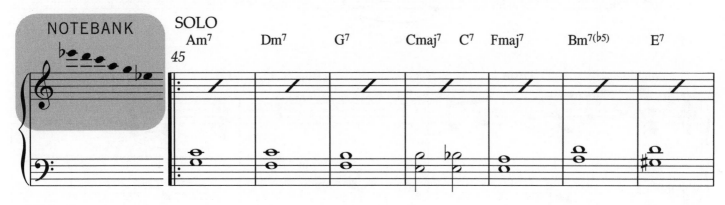

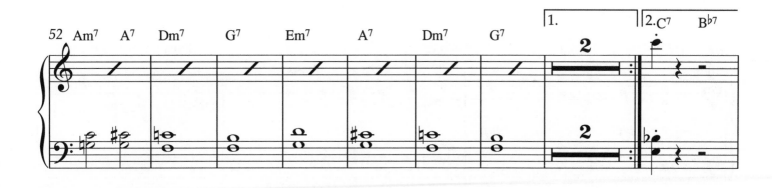

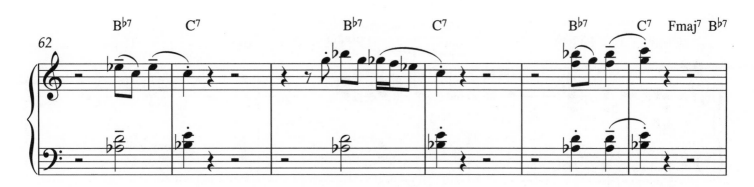

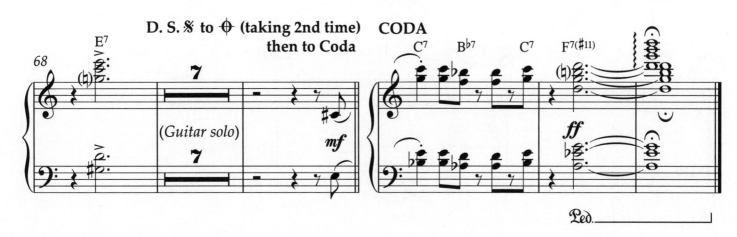

Song for Jo Alexander L'Estrange and Tom Pilling

to Coda SOLO

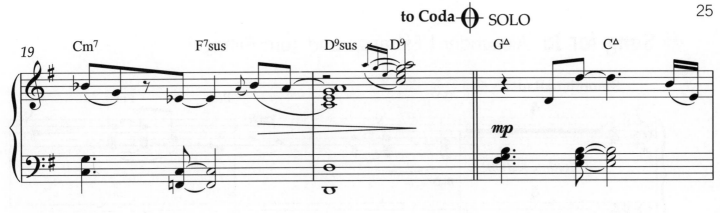

D. S. ℅ to ⊕ then to Coda   CODA

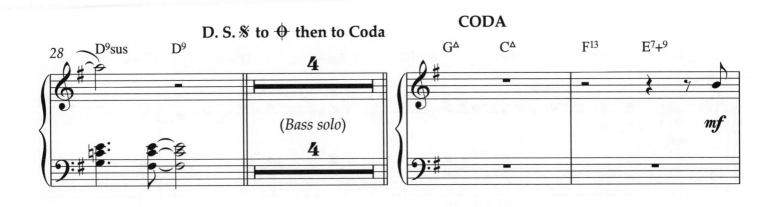

rall.

🎵 Song for Jo Alexander L'Estrange and Tom Pilling

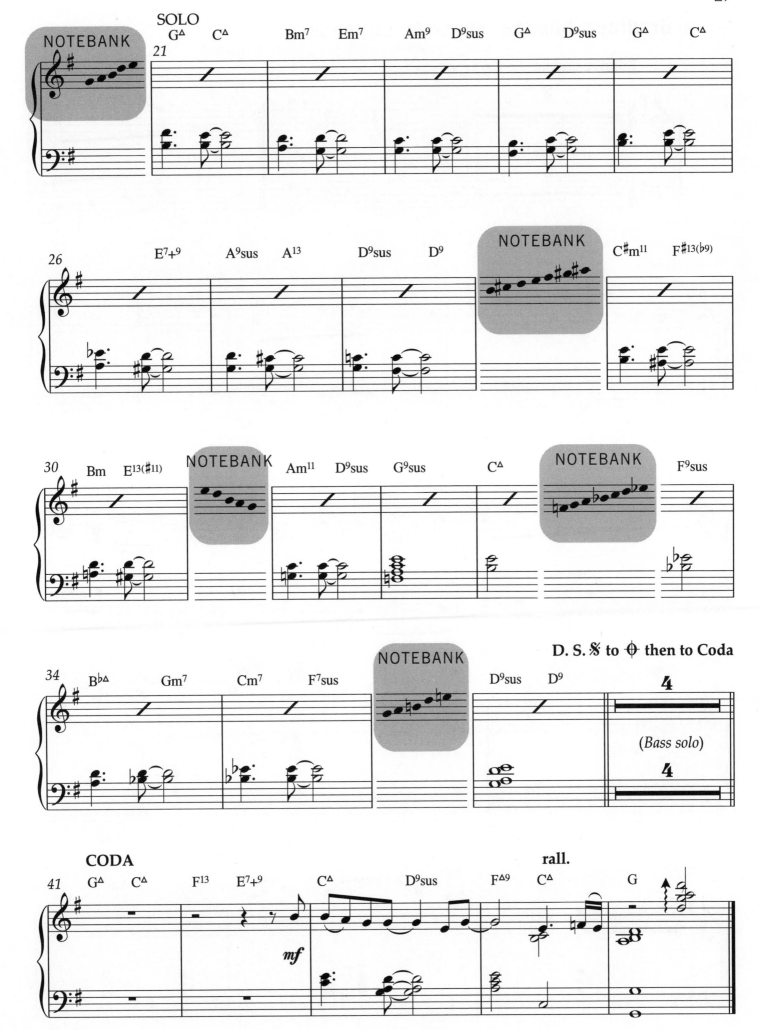

[13] **Bradley's bounce** Alexander L'Estrange

14 Bradley's bounce Alexander L'Estrange

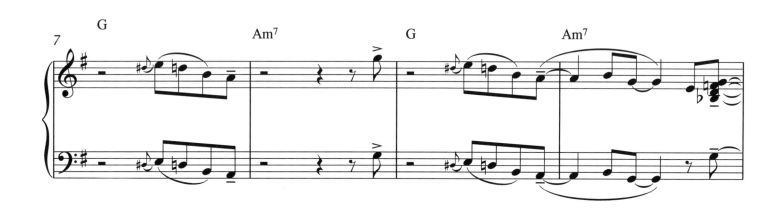

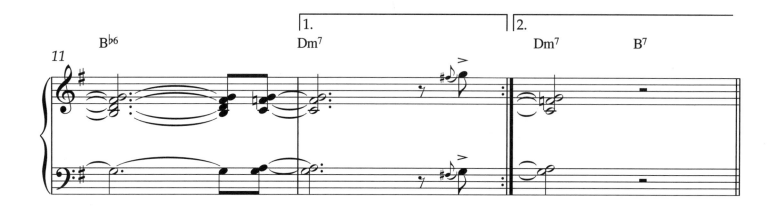

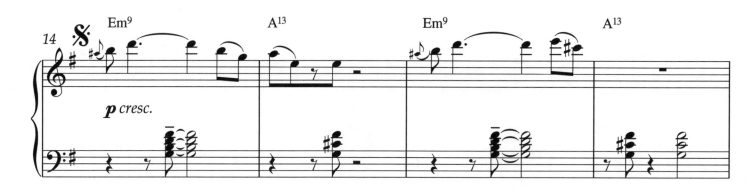

🄐 It's me, O Lord   traditional spiritual arr. L'Estrange and Pilling

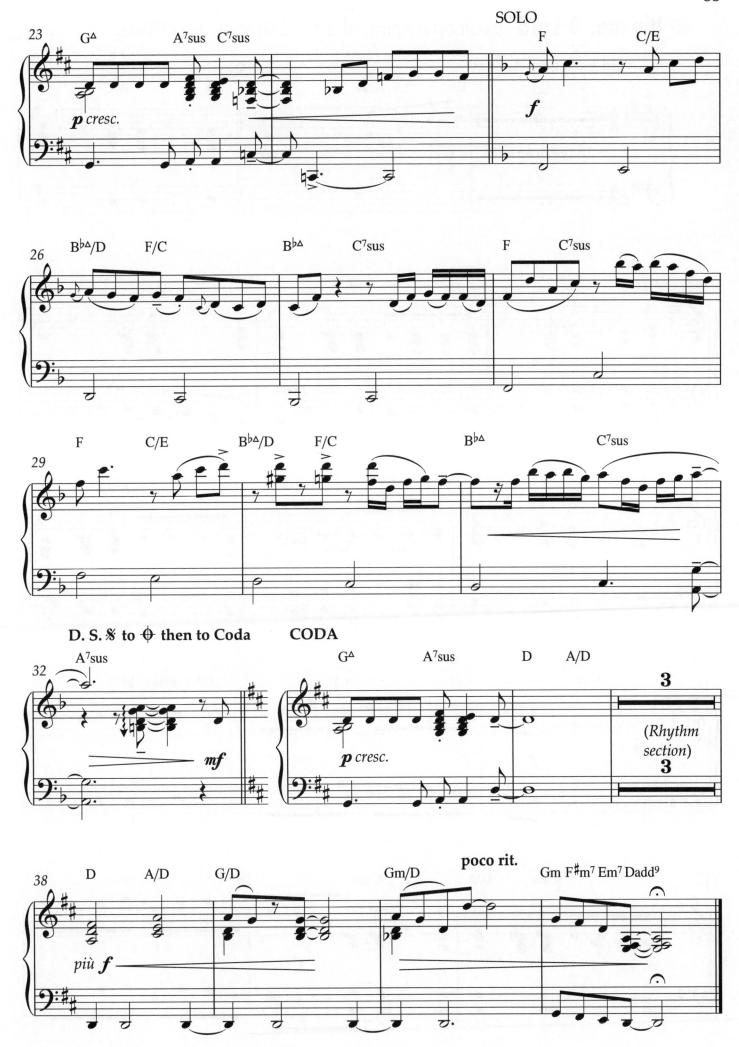

It's me, O Lord   traditional spiritual arr. L'Estrange and Pilling

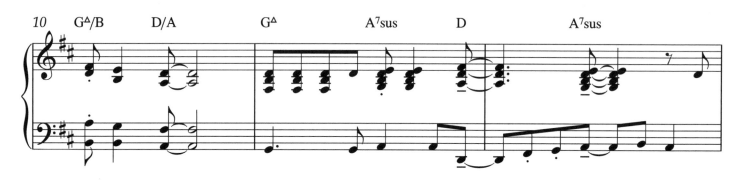

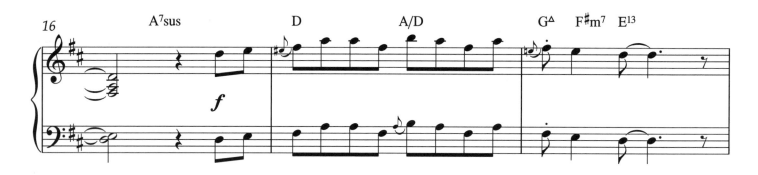

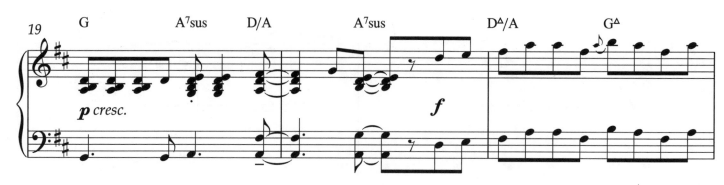

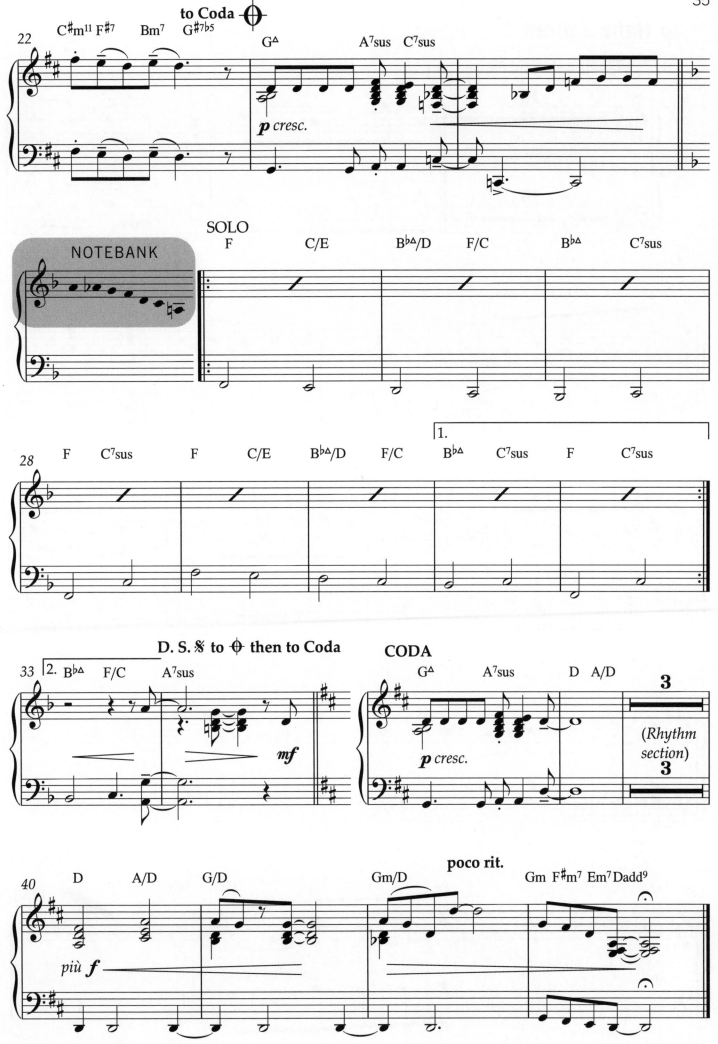

17 **Hafiz Zahran** Tom Pilling

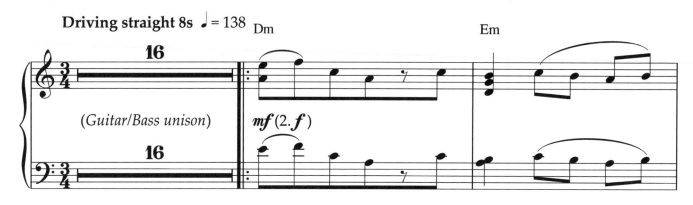

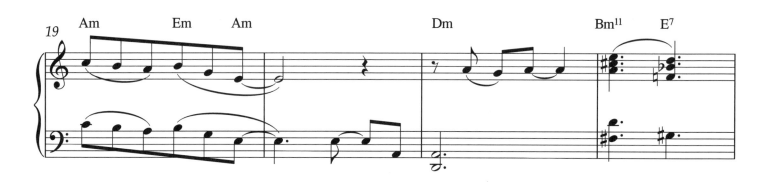

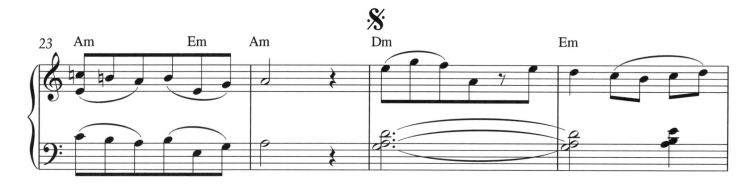

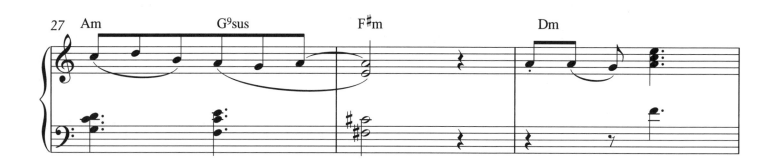

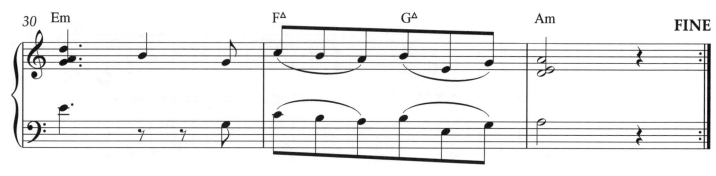

SOLO

D. S. % to Fine

Hafiz Zahran · Tom Pilling

NOTEBANK   SOLO

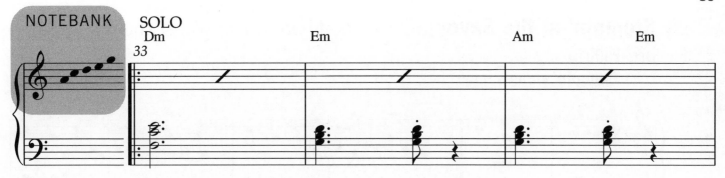

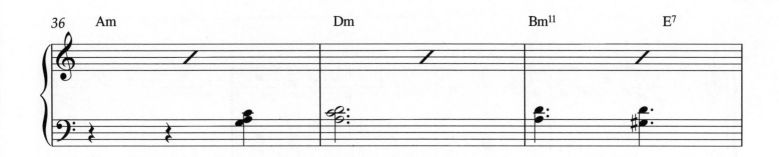

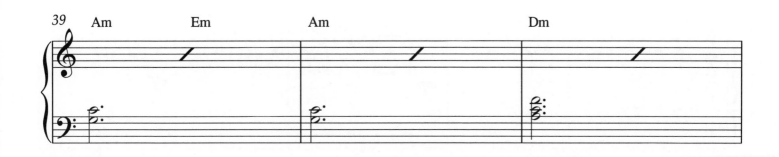

D. S. 𝄋 to Fine

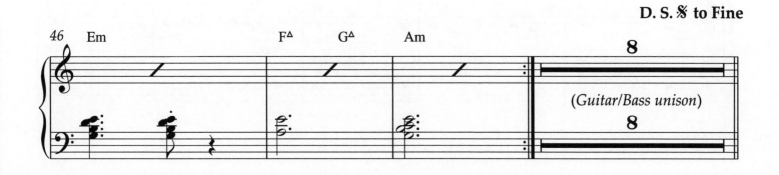

(Guitar/Bass unison)

Stompin' at the Savoy
Benny Goodman, Chick Webb and Edgar Sampson

arr. Pilling

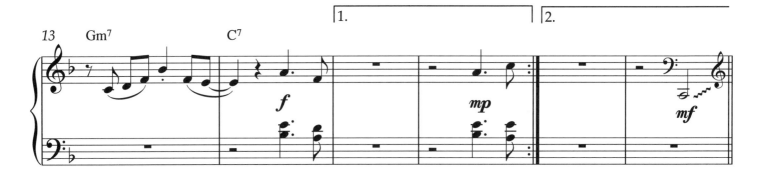

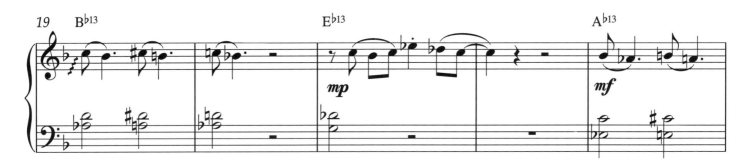

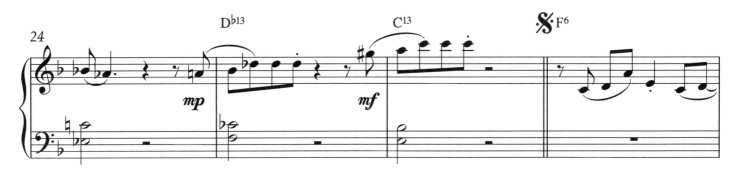

Stompin' at the Savoy
Benny Goodman, Chick Webb and Edgar Sampson

arr. Pilling

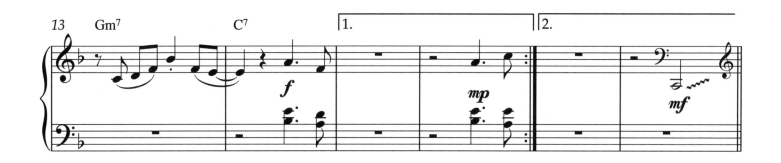

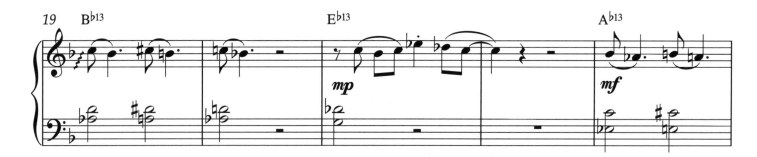

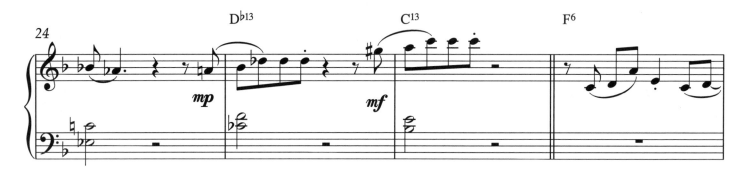

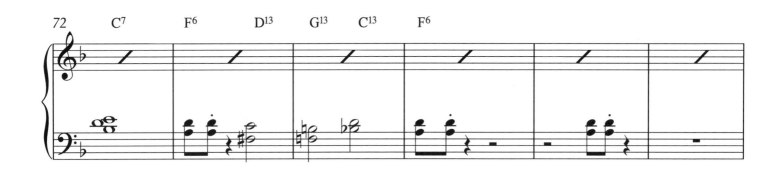

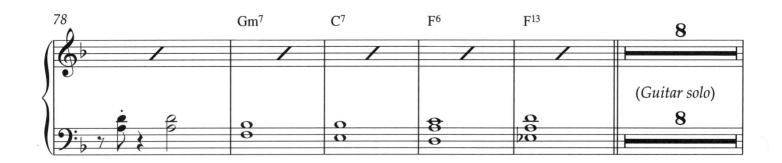

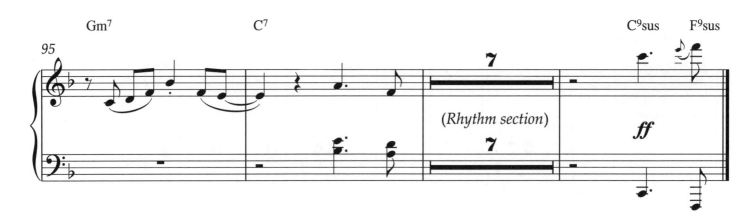